Paint
Effects

KEVIN TENNEY

MINI · WORKBOOK · SERIES

MEREHURST

CONTENTS

Crackled shelf (top left), verdigris candelabra (far left) and sponged-off wall (left)

What is a paint effect?

'Paint effect' is a term applied to any technique that goes beyond plain, solid colour painting. It still employs solid colour as the base coat but then adds one or more semi-transparent coats of paint, called glazes, over the base. These glazes are textured or broken open with a variety of tools (brushes, rags, combs etc) to create dimension and subtle movement of colour. This is the basic technique for paint effects and is known as 'broken colour'.

Broken colour techniques form the basis of 'faux finishes', a term often mentioned in decorative painting. Strictly speaking, the term applies to the imitation of a substance other than that on which you are painting. Examples include using paint to turn wood into a marble finish, or plaster into stone.

The basic techniques explained in this book are the starting point of all paint effects. Master each separately through practice and then apply them singly or in combination to give an individual signature to your own surroundings.

HISTORY
Paint effects may seem to have appeared only in recent years but, in fact, have been with us since prehistoric times when the cave dwellers used natural pigments on rock faces to record stories of their activities. For centuries the secrets of paint effect techniques were revealed only to craftsmen and professionals, but over the years and with the emergence of the current 'do-it-yourself' boom, this information is now available to all.

Paints, mediums, brushes and tools

If you're seriously taking up paint effects, collecting brushes, tools and mediums can become a lifetime habit. Start with the basic tools and brushes and gradually build up your collection.

PAINTS AND MEDIUMS

The projects covered in this book have all been completed using water-based paints and mediums. The great advantage of this is that fumes and toxicity are reduced to a minimum and cleaning of brushes and tools is easily done with water and detergent.

The colours used to create the individual paint finishes have been listed for each project though, depending on the project, you may want to choose your own colours.

PAINTS

Water-based house paints (emulsion and acrylic paints) are generally used as base coats for painted finishes and are available in such a vast range that it is seldom necessary to mix your own colour. They are available in a variety of finishes, including:

- matt emulsion
- silk emulsion
- water-based acrylic eggshell

For most paint effects projects you can use any of the above in a glaze, but will find it best to use silk emulsion or acrylic eggshell as a base coat. Paint with a sheen allows the glaze to be moved about on the surface: a surface paint in a matt finish would absorb the glaze quickly.

ARTISTS' ACRYLIC PAINTS

When it does become necessary to mix a shade you can't find in the paint shop, tubes of these intense colours are the solution. Blend them with water-based house paints for base colours; with house paint and/or scumble and water for glazes. Student grade paints are quite satisfactory when used as tints.

Thin the paints with a little water before adding to the paint/glaze. This helps to ensure complete mixing and avoids the possibility of a streak of pure colour appearing in your finish (straining the paints through discarded tights can prevent this).

UNIVERSAL TINTS

These tints are used by professional painters and in the colour mixing machines in paint shops but tend to be available only in large containers and are therefore expensive. As tints do not contain drying agent, they should not be used in a scumble and water-only glaze, except in small quantities.

SEALERS (WATER-BASED)

Applied to some bare surfaces to prevent absorption of top coats, sealers often have a milky appearance in the container but dry clear.

SCUMBLE MEDIUM

Also known as glaze medium, acrylic glaze or extender, scumble medium is the magic ingredient that makes paint effects possible. Scumble retards drying time, adds transparency and holds the impression of whatever tool is used in a particular finish.

GLAZES

The word 'glaze' in paint effects does not imply a degree of sheen—in fact, 'glazes' are almost always matt. Most glazes consist of equal parts of paint, scumble medium and water. It is good practice to mix the paint and scumble medium together before adding water. If a shiny finish is required to enhance or protect a particular technique, use a final coat of varnish or wax.

CRACKLE MEDIUM

Crackle medium is a clear, viscous coating that is sandwiched between layers of paint to produce cracks in the top coat. This finish must be protected with acrylic varnish as any moisture on the surface will reactivate the crackle medium.

LIMING GLAZE

You can use a glaze to achieve the effect of liming, which shows up the grain in bare timber. Alternatively, there are ready-mixed liming mediums available.

ACRYLIC VARNISH

Until recently, varnishes were made only in oil-based systems and tended to yellow with age. The new acrylic system reduces this to an absolute minimum, so it can be used even over pastel finishes. Available in matt, satin or gloss, water-based varnish is tough enough to be used on floors where several coats give sufficient protection to decorative paintwork. Acrylic varnish is milky in the container but dries completely clear.

METHYLATED SPIRITS

A solvent for dried water-based paints, methylated spirits will soften and remove paint if applied before the paint is fully cured. It is also used for cleaning stencils.

BRUSHES AND TOOLS

Always choose a brush of a size relative to the project at hand—big for walls, small for details.

DECORATING BRUSHES

The projects in this book require brushes for base coat and glaze but, if preferred, the one brush can be used to perform both functions.

Apply the base coat with the brush and, while the paint is drying, wash the brush and dry it. The same brush can then be used for applying the glaze (the brush should not be wet as a wet brush will make the glaze watery).

• The basic wall brush serves as a perfect brush for base coating and is available with black or white bristles about 100–125 mm (4–5 in) wide. The bristles should be as dense as possible to hold lots of paint so a large area can be covered quickly. The best quality brush has bristles with split ends to soften brush marks.

• Smaller brushes, 25–50 mm (1–2 in) wide, are generally used for painting woodwork, cutting-in edges in conjunction with rollers, and base coating small projects. Nylon brushes can be used for water-based paints.

• Foam brushes are also useful for painted finishes and are used to apply paints and mediums.

• Varnish brushes (flatter than normal paint brushes) should be kept solely for varnishing to avoid contamination of the varnish by small particles of paint.

ROLLERS

Rollers are useful when painting large areas but don't work too fast as this produces a fine spray. Small rollers can be used for stencilling.

ARTISTS' BRUSHES

Flat bristle brushes called fitches are used for dragging in small areas; the round version is used for stippling or stencilling. Pointed, round artists' brushes in hair or nylon (sizes 000 to 3) are ideal for fine freehand details and adding veins and cracks in marble.

WALL DRAGGERS

These brushes are expensive but much faster and more accurate for dragging large areas. As an alternative you can try a flogger or a wall brush.

STENCIL BRUSHES

The traditional stencil brush is round, short handled and cut totally flat. Round fitches may be used as substitutes but they are more difficult to use as they have slightly domed

Black bristle brush for base coat and glazes

Nylon brush for fine finishes and varnishes

Fitch brush (small) can be used for dragging

Artists' brush for veining (marbling) and detail work

Large wall brush for glazes and base coats

Flogger for dragging large areas such as walls

Wall dragger for covering large areas

Stencil brush *for applying paint through a stencil*

Wire brush *for raising the grain on wooden articles*

Small foam brush *for general painting and varnishing*

Metal comb

Plastic comb   ***Rubber comb***

Craft knife *for cutting stencils and general cutting*

Turkey feather *for marbling*

heads and so they give a more dense application of paint.

WIRE BRUSH
This brush has stiff, wire bristles and is used to open up the grain on timber before applying a finish.

FEATHERS
Goose or turkey feathers are the best for adding veins in marble and create an effect that cannot be replicated by any brush.

SPONGES
See the box on sponges, page 45.

RAGS
Well-washed cotton is best for paint finish techniques. Old sheets or shirts, fine upholstery calico or cheesecloth are all used dry for softening the glaze.

COMBS
Widely used in woodgraining, combs may be found in art supply stores (see the box on combs, page 18).

ABRASIVE PAPER
Abrasive paper is available in many grades. The most frequently used by decorative painters are medium/fine grade for general application and fine wet-and-dry for fine finishes or pieces that will be handled. Wet sanding is usually done between coats of varnish. After sanding, use a tack cloth to wipe away any dust.

LOW-TACK TAPES
See box on low-tack tapes, page 19.

General directions

Paint effect techniques can be performed on almost any surface and each needs to be adequately prepared. The success of any project depends on careful planning and preparation. It may seem the most tedious part of the exercise but it is well worth the effort.

PREPARATION OF SURFACES

Because the choice of water-based paints and mediums is now so wide, users should carefully follow the container directions of the chosen product. However, the following basic steps are common to every situation:

- All surfaces to be painted must be firm, clean and dry.
- Paints must be thoroughly stirred before and during application.
- Always allow recommended drying time between coats.
- Glossy surfaces must be sanded to ensure adhesion of top coats.

BARE SURFACES

The preparation required for most paint finishes will depend on the type of surface.

- Masonry, cement, plasterboard, plaster: Apply two coats of the base colour.
- Woodwork: Fill where necessary, apply a coat of sealer and then two coats of base colour.
- Metal: Apply an appropriate metal primer, then the base colour.
- Plastics and ceramics: Glossy surfaces must be given a 'key' to hold the paint. This is done by sanding the surface or applying a bonding medium such as a PVA adhesive. There are various proprietary bonding preparations now available. Apply the bonding medium and finish with two coats of base colour.

PREVIOUSLY PAINTED SURFACES

Wash down previously painted surfaces with detergent and water to remove dirt and grease.

- Masonry, cement, plasterboard, plaster: Fill and seal where necessary. Apply two coats of base colour.
- Woodwork: Smooth by sanding any chipped edges, fill and seal where necessary. Finish by applying two coats of base colour.
- Metal, plastics and ceramics: Treat these surfaces as for woodwork.

QUANTITIES OF PAINT

Most of today's house paints cover 12–14 m^2 (130–150 ft^2) per litre. For a glaze you will need considerably less paint: not only is glaze diluted with water and scumble medium but it is applied more thinly. Calculate the paint component in a glaze as about one quarter of the volume of one base coat.

A layer of blue paint crackled over a yellow base coat produces a colourful and contemporary look for this shelf.

Crackling

Crackling is one of the easiest paint effects to master, providing painted surfaces such as furniture, picture frames or this small shelf with an interesting surface texture. A crackle finish is achieved by applying a layer of crackle medium sandwiched between two coats of colour. As the top coat of paint dries, small cracks appear, exposing areas of the base colour.

MATERIALS

- Brush for base coat
- Water-based paint with a sheen: yellow, blue
- Low-tack masking tape (optional)
- Foam or bristle brush for crackle medium
- Crackle medium
- Foam or bristle brush for second colour
- Brush for varnish
- Water-based satin varnish

METHOD

1 Prepare the surface (see General directions, page 9).

2 Using the brush for the base coat, apply a coat of yellow paint to the piece. The paint must have a finish with a sheen to prevent absorption of the crackle medium. If necessary,

HINT

If you prefer the look of timber showing through the cracks rather than a painted base, omit step 2.

apply a second coat of paint to achieve an even coverage. When selecting paint colours, choose low contrast for a subtle effect; high contrast, as in this project, gives a more graphic look to the piece.

3 If desired, use low-tack masking tape to cover up any areas that you do not want to crackle, such as around the rim of the shelf or on the edge of the support brackets (see the box on low-tack tapes, page 19).

4 Using the foam or bristle brush, generously apply the crackle medium, keeping the application tool well loaded. While either a bristle or foam brush is suitable, a foam brush allows the medium to flow on easily. If using a bristle brush ensure the brush is well loaded—do not stretch the medium out or the crackled effect will be very minimal. Allow the medium to dry, preferably overnight.

5 Using a clean and dry bristle or foam brush, apply the top coat of blue paint. The paint must flow on

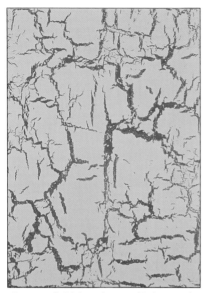

A coat of thick paint applied over the crackle medium will produce a large, graphic crack.

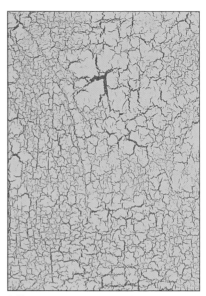

Thinning the paint slightly with water and applying the paint with a roller produces a finer crack.

REMOVING TAPE

If you have used low-tack masking tape to isolate any area, carefully cut around the tape with a sharp blade before removing it. The crackle medium will have formed a skin over the tape edge and could be lifted unless you take this precaution.

in a full coat and not be stretched out. The paint will crack in the direction of the application, so use crosshatching to avoid parallel cracks. As the paint dries, the crackle pattern will appear—the thicker the top coat of paint, the bigger the crack. For a finer crack, thin the paint slightly with water. Applying the paint with a lamb's-wool roller will also help achieve a fine crack. Again, keep the roller well loaded and work in a crisscross pattern, using very little pressure. Allow to dry and carefully remove the tape (see box alongside).

6 As this finish is fragile until it has matured, apply two coats of satin varnish to the piece, allowing the varnish to dry between each coat.

HINT

If you are working on a self-assembly piece such as this shelf, it is easier to complete the painting and crackling before the shelf is assembled.

CARE OF BRUSHES AND TOOLS

Protect your investment by proper cleaning of brushes and tools after every use. All water-based paints and mediums require only water and detergent or soap to clean them up. The golden rule is to remember to clean all brushes, sponges and tools as soon as possible after using them.

CLEANING BRUSHES AND ROLLERS

1 Rinse brushes in a bucket or under running water to remove the surplus paint. Rub some detergent or soap onto the brush, working it well into the bristles. Similarly, rollers should be washed well using water and detergent.

2 To soak brushes prior to final cleaning, suspend them in water using bulldog clips to hold the bristles clear of the bottom of the jar. Never allow a brush to rest on its bristles.

3 After soaking, rinse the brush again, squeeze out most of the water and shape the bristles with your fingers. Allow the brushes to dry by laying them flat over the edge of a shelf or table. Do not upend the brushes in a jar as this allows water to run back into the ferrule and damage the brush.

4 If you have allowed a brush to dry with water-based paint in it, soaking it in methylated spirits will usually soften the paint so you can wash it out in water.

STENCILS

Clean stencils by placing them flat on a pad of newspaper and gently rubbing them with a cloth wet with methylated spirits. As methylated spirits is a solvent for dried water-based paint, it is also useful for cleaning up splashes and errors—don't rub so hard that you go right through to the base coat.

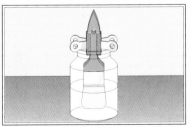

2 Suspend the brushes with bulldog clips to prevent the bristles from touching the bottom of the jar.

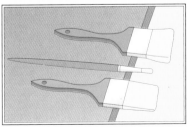

3 To dry the brushes, lay them flat with the bristles hanging over the edge of a shelf or table.

Distressing

The simplest way to create the look of 'aged' paintwork is to apply several layers of paint and then sand through them to reveal the different layers of colour underneath. The effect is enhanced by using three or more colours applied one on top of each other.

METHOD

1 If you are working on bare wood, apply one coat of sealer to the piece and allow it to dry. If using a previously painted or varnished chair, sand it lightly with medium grade abrasive paper. If the timber is previously painted in a colour you do not want to show, strip the piece completely and apply the sealer.

2 Using the bristle brush, evenly apply one coat of each of the three colours of water-based paint. Allow the paint to dry between each coat.

3 Start with the medium grade abrasive paper and sand back the top colour, particularly over areas that would normally receive the greatest wear (the chair rungs and front of the seat). Wipe off the dust with the tack cloth.

4 Using the fine grade abrasive paper, work all over the piece to expose the lower colours and even a little of the base timber.

5 Using the steel wool, soften any hard edges or scratches to produce a fine blending of all the colours. The top coat will remain dominant.

MATERIALS

- Water-based sealer
- Abrasive paper: one sheet each of fine and medium grade
- 25 mm (1 in) bristle brush
- Water-based paint with a sheen: pink, lavender, jade
- Tack cloth
- Steel wool: 0000 grade
- Brush for varnish
- Water-based satin varnish
- Furniture wax (optional)

6 Depending on the amount of wear the piece will receive, it can be left unvarnished or can be protected with a coat of satin varnish or furniture wax. If you are distressing a table top or a tray, it is best to protect the surface from further wear and tear by applying two to three coats of satin varnish (see the box on applying varnish, page 29).

HINT

To enhance the 'aged' effect, dint the surface with a hammer or a brick. Use a soft cloth to apply brown boot polish over the surface and wipe off the excess.

A three-colour distressing technique imparts a soft, well-worn appearance to this child's chair.

This trinket box uses a combination of wavy and geometrical combed patterns to produce quite a dramatic effect.

Combing

Combing originated as a technique to simulate woodgrain and was popular with nineteenth century American craftsmen. Today, combing can be used to create designs other than a woodgrain effect and can include bolder geometrical patterns such as the striking design used on this trinket box. The tool used for combing can be made from metal, plastic or cardboard, or you can even use an ordinary plastic hair comb.

METHOD

1 Prepare the surface (see General directions, page 9).

2 Using the small brush, apply two coats of chrome yellow acrylic paint to the piece, allowing the paint to dry between coats. Lightly sand the entire surface to ensure it is smooth—the comb must not hit any bumps or the combing pattern will be disturbed. Wipe away the dust with the tack cloth.

3 Make the glaze by mixing 1 part burnt sienna acrylic paint, 1 part scumble medium and 1 part water. Make sure the paint is thoroughly mixed in before adding water.

4 Using the brush for the glaze, apply a coat of brown glaze to the surface. Use a cotton rag to lightly dab over the wet glaze to soften the brush marks. If working on a larger piece, it is better to work on one surface at a time to ensure the glaze does not dry before it is combed.

MATERIALS

- Small brush for base coat
- Artists' acrylic paints: chrome yellow (base), burnt sienna (glaze)
- Abrasive paper: fine grade
- Tack cloth
- Acrylic scumble medium
- Brush for glaze
- Cotton rags
- Combing tool (see box on combs, page 18)
- Low-tack masking tape (optional)
- Brush for varnish
- Water-based satin varnish

3 Make the glaze by mixing the paint and scumble medium thoroughly and then adding the water.

COMBS

Combs are available from artists' supply stores in steel or rubber but you can cut your own from leather, cardboard or plastic. Steel combs require a greater level of expertise so it is best to graduate to them. The stiff plastic lids of food containers are simple to cut and use. For small pieces a comb about 75 mm (3 in) wide is ideal. Use sharp scissors or a craft knife to cut small V-shapes or teeth, spacing them 3 mm (⅛ in) apart. Don't make the teeth too big or paint may build up in the gaps and cause unevenness in the pattern.

Ensure the bottom edge is straight and leave a wide flange on the top edge as this makes the comb more rigid. Alternatively, for added strength, glue a strip of cardboard on the back above the teeth.

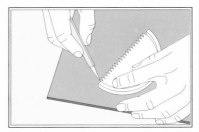

To make a comb, cut a plastic lid in half and cut small V-shaped notches along the edge.

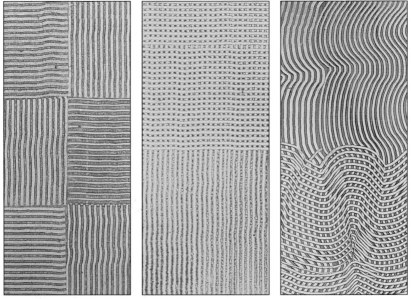

Various combing patterns and glaze colours can produce dramatic effects. Here blue, brown and green glazes have been combed over a yellow base coat using basketweave, crosshatch and wavy patterns.

5 With the comb in one hand and a cotton rag in the other, run the comb through the wet glaze to evenly reveal the base colour. Use moderate pressure and draw through without hesitation so the combing lines remain consistent. Wipe the excess paint from the comb onto the rag. Any pattern or direction is acceptable—straight lines, crosshatch, basketweave, waves, moiré or swirls—but experiment first on a sample board before committing to the final piece (see Sample boards, page 37). A more dramatic effect can be achieved by combining patterns such as waves with a straight geometrical pattern as used on this box.

6 To create the painted brown border around the box use low-tack tape to mask 5 mm (¼ in) borders around the lid and rim of the box (see box on low-tack tapes at right). Using a brush and the brown glaze, add the painted border. Allow it to dry and carefully remove the tape.

7 To complete the box apply two coats of satin varnish.

HINT

If you are not happy with your combed pattern or you make a mistake, reload the brush with glaze and quickly paint over the combing. As the glaze remains wet for a short time, you will be able to paint over your mistake and begin the combing again.

LOW-TACK TAPES

Low-tack tapes are less likely to remove the base coat where you have masked off than ordinary masking tape. Painter's tape is ideal but if you use the normal white crepe paper masking tape, reduce its tack slightly by pressing it against your clothing or other fabric. Be careful that you do not reduce the tack too much or the paint will bleed under the tape. Never apply tape to a surface that is not thoroughly dry and always run a thumb nail along the edge to ensure the tape is sticking well to prevent paint leaking under it.

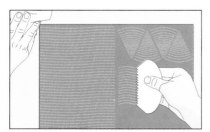

5 Comb various patterns in the wet glaze. Practise on a sample board before committing to the project.

6 Mask the rim of the box using low-tack tape and add a painted border using the brown glaze.

Malachite combing

The pattern and colours used in this combing technique are inspired by malachite, a mineral containing swirling bands of blue-green, dark green and white. This placemat shows a simplified version using a green glaze over a black background.

METHOD

1 Prepare the surface (see General directions, page 9). Make a combing tool (see box on combs, page 18) but for the malachite combing technique, cut the teeth in irregular widths and vary the spacing.

2 Base coat the placemats with two coats of black paint. Sand the surface lightly and wipe away the dust.

3 Use the low-tack tape to mask off a 3 cm (1¼ in) border.

4 Mix the glaze using 1 part pthalo green, 1 part Hooker's green and a touch of white to produce a bright blue-green paint. Mix 1 part blue-green paint, 1 part scumble medium and 1 part water to make the glaze.

MATERIALS

- Small brush for base coat
- Artists' acrylic paints: black, pthalo green, Hooker's green, white, ultramarine blue
- Abrasive paper: fine grade
- Tack cloth
- Low-tack masking tape
- Acrylic scumble medium
- Brush for glaze
- Cotton rags
- Combing tool (see Combs, page 18)
- Brush for varnish
- Water-based satin varnish

5 Apply a coat of the glaze to the base coated surface. Fold a cotton rag into a wad and gently dab it over the painted surface to break up any brush marks.

6 With the combing tool in one hand and a rag in the other, draw through the glaze using moderate pressure. Wipe the excess paint from the comb onto the rag. The malachite pattern is a series of overlapping swirls and wavering curves—no straight lines. (An illustrated book on minerals may be a useful reference.) Use the edge of an eraser to create some thicker lines.

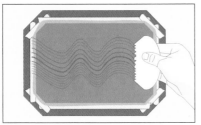

6 Use the combing tool to create wavy lines through the wet glaze. Wipe the excess glaze off the comb.

The malachite finish on this placemat uses black as the base colour; try using white to achieve a different effect.

Allow the glaze to dry and carefully remove the masking tape.

7 Mask off the painted central area and a 1 cm (⅜ in) border and then add the blue border.

8 Allow the paint to dry thoroughly and remove the masking tape. To finish, apply at least two to three coats of satin varnish. Items which will receive a lot of wear, should be varnished with three coats.

The stencilled motif running along this wall is created using a two-part stencil. The geometric design is complemented by the delicate combination of the cream and mauve striped sponging beneath it.

Stencilling

The use of stencils is a simple way of introducing a decorative element into an interior. Alone, or in combination with other techniques such as sponging or ragging, stencilling gives a totally different look to a room.

MATERIALS

- Clear adhesive tape
- Stencil plastic
- Fine line permanent marker
- Metal ruler
- Scissors
- Cutting mat
- Scalpel or small craft knife
- Nail punch
- Spirit level
- Chalk
- Low-tack masking tape
- Artists' acrylic paints: Prussian blue, diox purple, crimson, white
- Five shallow paint containers
- Five 2 cm (¾ in) stencil brushes
- Paper towels

PREPARATION

1 Stencils can be applied to almost any wall surface with any water-based paint. Prepare the surface (see General directions, page 9).

CUTTING THE STENCILS

2 Photocopy the designs for Stencil A and Stencil B, located on pages 62–3, making the stencils as small or large as desired. If necessary, tape the photocopies together so that you have more than three repeats of the star for both stencils.

3 Cut the stencil plastic to size, allowing at least 5 cm (2 in) around the design to protect the background when applying the paint. Using the permanent marker and ruler, draw a horizontal line through the centre of the film and cut V-shaped notches on this line at the film edge. These are later lined up on a chalk line.

4 Lay the photocopy for Stencil A face down on the stencil plastic, matching the centre line to the one you've drawn. Tape the photocopy in position. Turn over the stencil plastic so you can see the design through it. You are now ready to cut the stencil.

CUTTING STENCILS

Self-healing cutting mats are ideal for cutting stencils but a thick pad of newspaper or heavy cardboard provides an ideal substitute. Avoid heavy, bulky craft knives as they are more tiring to use than a scalpel or special stencil cutter.

5 Hold the craft knife like a pen and use just enough pressure to cut the stencil plastic—relax your grip and draw a fluid line with the blade. Use a steel ruler to cut straight lines and a nail punch for small round holes. It's best to leave the border lines until last to prevent movement in the stencil plastic. Remove and discard the photocopy when the stencil is cut. Repeat this process using the design for Stencil B.

STENCILLING

6 If stencilling onto a wall, use a spirit level to draw a chalk line where the centre line of Stencil A will be on the wall, usually about 95 cm (3 ft) above the floor. Lining up the notches in the stencil with the line, tape the stencil to the wall. Use low-tack tape as ordinary masking tape may damage the wall. If stencilling onto a flat surface such as a table, draw the line with chalk and ruler.

7 Prepare the paints for stencilling. Add a few drops of water to each colour to bring them to a heavy cream consistency. Be careful: too

---

STENCILLING FRIEZES

When stencilling long lines or strips, fade out as you approach the end of the cut rather than creating a hard edge and blend in where the second stencil overlaps.

---

much water and they will run under the edges of the stencil. In this project, white was added to the Prussian blue and purple to create lighter shades of each. The paints will go a long way so you only need about a quarter of a cup of each—put the paints into shallow containers.

8 Dip the stencil brush into the first colour (see Hint, page 25). Dab the brush onto a pad of paper towels to remove the excess paint and to evenly spread the paint. The brush should leave just a light film of colour on the paper. Holding the brush at right angles to the wall and using an up-and-down dabbing motion, lightly fill the stencil cuts in the central star. Work from the outside edges of the stencil towards the middle, ensuring there is an even coverage of paint.

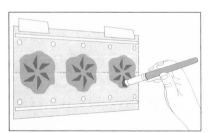

8 Working with a circular dabbing motion, apply the paint through the cut areas of the stencil.

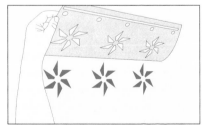

9 Carefully lift the stencil to check the first print. You may need to repeat the stencilling to darken the colour.

Stencil A is taped into position on the wall and the first colours applied.

Stencil B is aligned over Stencil A and the stencilled design is completed.

9 At the end of the first colour, carefully lift the stencil to check your progress. You may find that you need to add more paint.

10 Complete Stencil A using a different stencil brush for each colour. Where there is only a small space between colours, use an offcut of stencil plastic to create a mask.

Carefully remove the stencil from the wall and allow the paint to dry. Line up and tape Stencil B in position and stencil as explained in steps 8–10.

11 Move Stencil A along the chalk line, laying the left-hand star cuts over the right-hand print to maintain even spacing. Continue to stencil along the length of the wall.

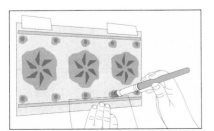

10 Use a piece of stencil plastic to act as a mask when stencilling near other small areas.

HINT

When stencilling, never use the brush directly from the pot of paint—you only need to use a very small amount of paint on the tip of the brush. If the brush begins to clog, rub it into a piece of damp cloth. Never use a wet brush to stencil as this will dilute the paint.

Marbling

This is one of the easiest marbling techniques to achieve though it is a good idea to practise on a sample board first before committing to your piece. The trick is not to add too many veins—this will only detract from the authenticity you are trying to achieve.

PREPARATION

1 If you are using bare wood, apply one coat of water-based sealer to the piece before commencing. If you are marbling on other surfaces, refer to General directions, page 9.

2 Using the brush for the base coat, apply two coats of black acrylic paint to the surface. Allow the paint to dry thoroughly between each coat.

3 If you want to add the contrasting border, the area must first be masked off. If the piece you are using is square, use low-tack masking tape to mask off a border approximately 4 cm (1½ in) wide. If the piece is round, such as this serving platter, use stencil plastic or card to create a mask.

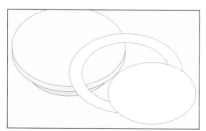

3 Cut two masks from stencil plastic or card: one circle the full diameter and one around 4 cm (1½ in) smaller.

To cut the circular masks, draw two circles on the card: one circle to the full diameter and a smaller circle, about 4 cm (1½ in) narrower, for the inner circle mask. Using the craft knife and mat, carefully cut out the inner and outer circles.

The illusion of a marbled surface can be created using paints, a feather and a fine brush. The black marbled finish on the centre of this serving platter is complemented by a sponged green border.

4 Using the mask for the outer border, position it onto the wood. Secure the mask in place with small pieces of adhesive putty.

MARBLING

5 Work on the marbling in the centre of the piece first. Mix a glaze of equal parts of white paint, scumble medium and water.

6 Wet the sea sponge with water and wring it out as much as possible. Pick up a little of the white glaze and run a few drifts of colour across the background. Immediately blot and soften with the cotton rag so that only a faint impression remains.

7 Run the outside edge of the feather between your fingers to ruffle it slightly, then dip it lightly into the white glaze. Draw the edge of the feather across the surface, varying the pressure and direction slightly as you go. Blot out with the rag in some areas to give the impression of the vein dropping below the surface: do not break it completely. Add just a few more random veins, avoiding

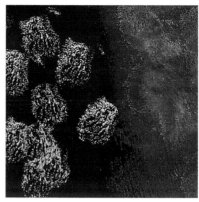

The glaze is sponged onto the surface and then a rag is used to blot and soften the sponged areas.

right angles and perfect parallels. The fewer the veins, the more convincing the marble will look.

8 Load the small brush with the glaze and intensify the white veins in some areas. This brush is also used to introduce fine cracks into the marble. Holding it with the handle tip between the thumb and first finger, draw in a few fine cracks, rotating the brush slightly. Corrections can be made by carefully wiping them out with a damp rag. Allow it to dry.

7 Dip the feather in the white glaze and draw the edge of the feather across the surface, varying the pressure.

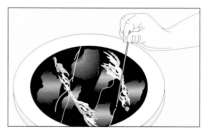

8 Holding the small brush by the tip, introduce smaller veins and fine cracks into the marbling.

Smaller veins and cracks are added to the finished sponged surface to add authenticity to the marble.

THE BORDER

9 To paint the border, remove the outer mask and cover the marbled area in the centre with the inner circle mask.

The sponged green border around the serving platter complements the central black marbled area.

10 Mix some of the chromium green oxide paint with water to achieve a creamy consistency and add it to the white paint in three containers to create light, mid and dark green.

11 Beginning with the darkest green, lightly sponge over the black base coat leaving some of the background showing. Turning to a fresh area of the sponge, repeat with the other greens, always allowing some of each colour to show. Do not overblend or the colours will become 'muddy'. Carefully remove the central mask and allow the work to dry overnight.

12 Apply at least two coats of satin varnish to your work. This not only protects the piece but increases the illusion of depth in the marble. Sand lightly between coats.

APPLYING VARNISH

Varnish can be a difficult medium to apply. Try this method to obtain a smooth finish free of brush marks. Apply the varnish with a mohair roller and immediately work over it with a large stipple brush. Allow the varnish to dry thoroughly and sand lightly with fine abrasive paper. Repeat the process several times. On a large area such as a table top, two people are needed for this method—one rolling the varnish onto the surface and one stippling.

Mahogany woodgraining

Re-creating the rich colours and textures of wood can be achieved by a simple yet effective woodgraining technique. Transparent glazes are applied over an appropriate base colour and a paint brush is used to create the 'grain'. The colours and technique used for this project create a mahogany straight grain.

METHOD

1 If you are working on bare, unpainted wood, the surface must first be sealed. Apply a coat of sealer to the wood and allow it to dry. If you are using previously painted or varnished wood, clean and sand the wood and wipe away the dust with a tack cloth.

2 Using the small brush for the base coat, apply two coats of nectarine base colour to the surface, allowing it to dry thoroughly between coats.

3 Make up the mahogany glaze. First mix equal quantities of burnt sienna,

MATERIALS

- Water-based sealer
- Abrasive paper: fine grade
- Tack cloth
- Small brush for base coat
- Water-based paint with a sheen: nectarine (base)
- Artists' acrylic paints: burnt sienna, raw umber, alizarin crimson
- Acrylic scumble medium
- Soft white bristle or nylon brush
- Stiff black bristle brush
- Cotton rags
- Brush for varnish
- Water-based satin varnish

The glaze has been applied over a nectarine base coat, and while still wet, a stiff brush is drawn through the glaze to create the 'woodgrain'.

raw umber and alizarin crimson acrylic paints to create the glaze colour. Mix 1 part glaze colour, 1 part scumble medium and 1 part water to create the mahogany glaze.

4 Apply the mahogany glaze to the surface in a crisscross pattern using the soft white bristle or nylon brush. It is best to practise the woodgraining technique on a board before committing to the project. (While a stiff brush creates an effective

A mahogany glaze is brushed over this skirting board and then wiped through with a stiff bristle brush to create the appearance of wood grain.

woodgrain there are also combs and tools designed specifically for creating a woodgrained finish. These can be purchased from most art and craft stores.)

5 Using a dry, stiff black bristle brush, immediately pull it through the wet glaze, creating a slightly wavy pattern as you go. Hold a cotton rag in the other hand and wipe the paint off the brush after every stroke. Allow the glaze to dry.

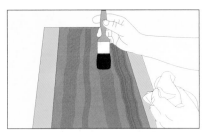

6 Apply heavier areas of glaze with the side of the brush and then soften the glaze with the flat of the brush.

6 Using the side of the black bristle brush, apply some heavier areas of the glaze. Turn the brush flat and pull through the glaze, wiping the excess paint off the brush. This will give depth of colour to the wood graining. Allow the glaze to dry.

7 Apply a final coat of glaze over the work. This coat may be slightly thinned with water to increase transparency. Brush out the glaze evenly and allow it to dry.

8 Apply two coats of satin varnish to give depth to the woodgraining as well as provide protection. This is particularly important on areas such as this skirting board that will be subject to a lot of wear.

FAUX MAHOGANY GRAINING VARIATION

To achieve a different look, try this faux mahogany variation, very popular in early American decoration. This is a very naive rendering of mahogany which looks great on country pieces.
To start, base coat the piece using deep pink (Cadmium red plus a little white). Mix the glaze using 1 part black paint, 1 part scumble medium and 2 parts water. Brush the glaze over the surface and then rag the glaze, following the technique described in the hint above. Allow large areas of the pink base coat to show through. Apply two coats of satin varnish.

Bird's eye maple graining

Maple graining is a simple woodgrain finish that is useful for decorating frames and small pieces. You need to work quickly while the glaze is wet to create the small 'bird's eye' pattern.

METHOD

1 Prepare the surface for graining (see step 1, page 30).

2 Base coat the surface using white or cream paint and allow the paint to dry overnight.

3 Mix a glaze of 1 part paint (raw umber plus a little burnt umber), 1 part scumble medium and 1 part water. Apply the glaze using broad strokes. Draw the brush through the glaze in straight lines, allowing it to hesitate every now and again to create light and darker areas.

4 Use the tip of your little finger to add in the 'bird's eye' markings. Scatter the 'eyes' about—some in tight

MATERIALS

- Water-based paint with a sheen for background: white or cream
- Small brush for base coat and glaze
- Artists' acrylic paint: raw umber, burnt umber
- Acrylic scumble medium
- Brush for varnish
- Water-based satin varnish

groups and some single eyes linking the groups. The glaze will flow slightly and soften the graining before it dries.

5 Allow the glaze to dry overnight and apply two coats of satin varnish. This will create the impression of depth in the 'timber'.

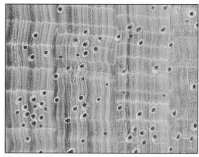

The brush has been allowed to waver slightly and hesitate randomly as it draws through the glaze.

The surface of the wet glaze has been lightly touched with a fingertip to create the 'bird's eyes'.

While a verdigris finish is usually associated with metal objects such as this candelabra, it can also work beautifully on items such as garden statues, plant pots or lamp bases.

Verdigris

Verdigris means 'green-grey' and is a popular paint finish that simulates the natural weathering which occurs on copper, bronze and brass. While a true verdigris finish develops after years of exposure to the elements, decorators can re-create the effect by a clever use of acrylic paints.

METHOD

1 When painting on bare metal, apply a metal primer to ensure the paint adheres to the surface. If painting on other surfaces, see General directions on page 9.

2 Using the small brush, apply two coats of black as the background colour. Allow the paint to dry.

3 Make up three glazes. First mix pthalo green with a small amount of raw umber to create the basic paint colour. Add more white to the basic paint colour to produce three varying degrees of green—dark, mid and light green. To make the three glazes, mix equal parts of green paint, scumble medium and water.

MATERIALS

- Small brush for base coat
- Water-based paint with a sheen: black (base coat)
- Artists' acrylic paints: pthalo green, raw umber, white
- Small round stencil brush (to apply glazes)
- Medium round stencil brush (for blending glazes)
- Cotton rags
- Brush for varnish
- Water-based flat varnish (optional)

The verdigris finish is composed of three green glazes—dark, mid and light green.

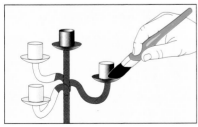

2 Use the small brush to apply two coats of black paint to the candelabra and allow the paint to dry.

The three green glazes are blended together to create the verdigris effect.

4 Using the small stencil brush, randomly apply patches of the darkest green over the background, leaving large areas of black still showing. While still wet, repeat with the two lighter greens, slightly overlapping the colours but still being able to see small areas of the black background. It is a good idea to practise your verdigris technique on a board or piece of paper before committing to the final piece (see Sample boards, page 37).

5 Holding the stencil brush vertically, blend the colours together. Practise on a sample board first.

5 Using the medium stencil brush, blend the three colours together. When stippling, hold the stencil brush so that it is vertical to the surface. Using an up-and-down movement, dab the bristles into the wet glaze to soften and blend the colours. Holding a rag in one hand, gently blend the colours together, constantly cleaning the paint out of the brush with the rag. Continue to gently dab the brush until the desired effect is achieved. Do not overblend the colours or you will finish up with plain green.

6 Unless the piece will receive a lot of wear and tear, it is preferable to leave this finish unvarnished, the flat chalky appearance being suggestive of the natural patina of verdigris. If necessary, apply one or two coats of flat varnish.

HINTS

• If you are painting on brass, omit the black background. Apply the three green glazes and following step 5, stipple to blend them. Wipe out some areas of the paint with a soft cloth to expose a little of the metal underneath.

• When using water-based paints over lacquered or highly polished surfaces, you may find the paint beads and will not cover the surface. Add a few drops of household detergent to the paint—this breaks the surface tension and allows the paint to cover.

PEWTER METALLIC PAINT FINISH

Paint effects need not only tranform metal objects such as the verdigris candelabra but with just a little imagination and creative flair can transform wooden or plaster blanks or pieces which need a face lift into items that have the appearance of metal. Try this pewter metallic finish on a wooden candlestick.

1 Sand the wood and brush away the dust with a tack cloth. Apply a coat of sealer and allow it to dry.

2 Base coat the entire piece using silver acrylic paint and allow the paint to dry.

3 Mix a glaze of 1 part scumble medium, 1 part water and 1 part black paint and apply it to the candlestick using a bristle brush.

4 Use a slightly damp cloth to wipe off some of the black glaze to expose small areas of the silver underneath.

5 Use a small stipple brush to dab over the surface to remove any brush marks and soften the edges where the silver is exposed.

6 Allow to dry and apply a coat of satin varnish to finish.

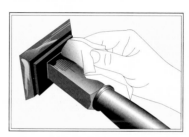

4 Use a damp cloth to wipe off the excess black glaze to expose areas of the silver base coat.

SAMPLE BOARDS

Before undertaking a new paint effect you should practise on a sample board before committing yourself to the final piece. A sample board can be made from foamcore or thin hardboard. To make the board, base coat the board with one or two coats of white paint, using a paint with a sheen. Alternatively, a coat of gloss varnish may be applied over a matt base coat to achieve the same result.

Now you can practice different paint effects on the same sample board, wiping off the paint with a damp rag after each application. Because the board has a glossy finish, the paint can easily be wiped off and the board can be used again and again in this manner.

Liming

Liming is a traditional technique, best suited to open-grained timbers such as oak, maple, pitch pine, elm and ash. In earlier times, floors and furniture were treated with a wash of real lime to prevent damage by insects. Today a paint finish simulates this.

MATERIALS

- Wire brush (optional)
- Water-based sealer
- Satin finish water-based paint: white
- Acrylic scumble medium
- Small bristle brush for glaze
- Cotton rags
- Brush for varnish
- Water-based satin varnish (optional)

METHOD

1 The wood to be limed must be new and untreated or if it has been previously painted, it must be stripped and wire-brushed to remove any ingrained finish; the wire brush also 'opens' the grain. Apply a coat of sealer to prevent the liming glaze from being absorbed into the wood.

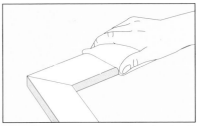

4 Fold a rag into a pad and wipe it over the surface to remove the excess liming medium.

2 Mix a liming glaze with equal parts of white paint and scumble medium.

3 Using the bristle brush, apply the white glaze over the whole surface, pushing the glaze well into the grain or any carved details in the wood.

4 Fold a cotton rag up to make a pad and gently wipe over the surface, first across the grain and then with it. Remove most of the glaze, leaving only a fine film with a heavier residue in the grain. Allow the glaze to dry thoroughly. To achieve a stronger intensity of liming repeat this process. Allow the glaze to dry overnight.

5 If the limed surface will be subject to wear and tear, apply two coats of satin varnish.

WAXING

As an alternative to using varnish, you may use wax as a finish on most paint work. While not durable enough for a floor, the wax will give a soft patina on furniture and decorative pieces. Limed surfaces are especially suited to waxing.

A limed paint effect looks particularly good on an open-grained timber such as that used for this picture frame. The liming glaze can accumulate in the recesses of the grain.

Rag rolling-off

Rag rolling-off is a very simple two-colour technique where the rag is folded into a sausage shape and then rolled onto a wet, glazed surface. This removes areas of the glaze creating a lovely soft texture, perfect for enhancing walls or furniture.

METHOD

1 All broken colour finishes are best performed over a semi-gloss base colour to slow absorption and allow movement of the paint. Prepare the surface as described in General directions on page 9.

2 Using the large brush for the base coat, apply two coats of yellow base colour and allow the paint to dry.

3 Make the glaze by mixing 1 part mushroom paint, 1 part scumble medium and 1 part water.

4 Using the glaze brush, apply the glaze in panels about 1 m (3 ft) wide, working from top to bottom.

5 Loosely roll and twist a soft cotton rag into a sausage shape. Depending on the size of the project, you may need to use several rags, each about 50 cm (20 in) square. Using both hands, roll the rag over the wet glaze. Move the rag about as you would a rolling pin maintaining fairly even pressure. You may want to practise your technique on a sample board first (see sample boards on page 37). Don't work the paint too much

MATERIALS
• Large brush for base coat
• Water-based paint with a sheen: chrome yellow (base), mushroom (glaze)
• Acrylic scumble medium
• Large brush for glaze
• Soft cotton rags (cheesecloth, fine upholsterer's calico or muslin)

or you may finish with bald patches. Fade out as you come to the edge of the glaze, then blend into the second panel. This is to prevent visible overlaps occurring where you finish one panel and begin the next one.

6 As the rags fill with glaze, discard them into a bucket of water and use a fresh one. A dry rag removes less

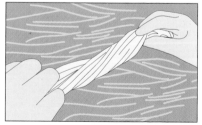

5 Loosely twist the rag into a sausage shape and roll it over the wet mushroom glaze.

The charm of this rag-rolled wall has been heightened by the addition of a rose stencil. (The pattern is on page 61.)

glaze and leaves a crisper impression than a damp one.

7 On walls or other large areas, this technique requires two people. The first person brushes the glaze over the base coat, the second follows closely behind working with the rag on the wet glaze. You do need to work quickly on all wall finishes before the panel edges dry out and leave faint lines down the wall.

This wall, sponged using an ultramarine blue glaze, certainly makes an impact. Bright colours such as these are excellent for decorating feature walls.

Sponging-off

Sponging-off is a broken colour technique where wet glaze is removed with a damp sea sponge. On the wall shown here, a dark blue glaze was applied over a light mushroom base coat. While the glaze was still wet it was sponged off to reveal glimpses of the base colour.

METHOD

1 Prepare the surface for the sponged paint finish (see General directions, page 9).

2 Using the large brush for the base coat, apply two coats of mushroom base colour to the surface and allow it to dry. The base colour will be slightly visible through the sponged layers, so, depending on taste, you may want to use a contrasting colour or one that tones in well with the sponged layers.

3 Make the sponging glaze by mixing 1 part blue paint, 1 part scumble medium and 1 part water.

4 Wet the sponge in water and squeeze it out as dry as possible before applying it to the paint.

5 If working on a large area such as a wall, the sponging-off technique requires two people—the first to apply the glaze, the second to remove the glaze with the sponge. Using the large brush for the glaze, apply the glaze in broad strokes in panels about 1 m (3 ft) wide.

6 Use the damp sponge to soften and remove some of the glaze. Keep the sponge moving and try to vary the direction of your hand to avoid repetition of the sponged design. As the sponge becomes filled with glaze drop it into water, squeeze out the excess water and continue. Keep a cloth nearby to dab up any paint runs down the wall.

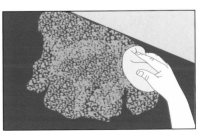

6 When sponging-off, use the damp sponge to soften and remove some of the wet glaze.

Two layers of sponged glazes usually work better than one. This wall uses blue and yellow glazes, or, for a less dramatic effect, try using two or three shades of the one colour.

Sponging-on

Sponging-on produces a crisp, mottled texture that is perfect for decorating large areas such as walls or provides an interesting finish on pots, boxes or furniture. Sponging-on, or applying glaze with a sponge, looks most effective when two or three glazes are sponged over the base coat.

METHOD

1 Prepare the surface (see General directions, page 9).

2 Using the large brush, apply two coats of the mushroom base colour to the surface and allow it to dry. The base colour will be slightly visible through the sponged layers so, depending on taste, you may want to use a contrasting colour or one that tones in well with the sponged layers.

SEA SPONGES

• There are various sizes of sea sponges available. Choose a large sponge for walls or larger pieces of furniture and a smaller one for pots or decorative items.
• Synthetic sponges create a much harsher outline and generally should be avoided.
• To prevent paint build-up during work, drop the sponge into a bucket of water. Squeeze out as much water as possible before re-applying it to the painted surface. At the end of work, wash it thoroughly in detergent and water, rinse and allow it to dry.

MATERIALS

• Large brush for base coat
• Water-based paint with a sheen: mushroom (base); ultramarine blue, yellow (glazes)
• Acrylic scumble medium
• Natural sea sponge

3 Make the first sponging glaze by mixing 1 part paint, 1 part scumble medium and 1 part water.

4 Wet the sponge in water and squeeze it out as dry as possible before putting it into the paint.

5 Pour the glaze into a roller tray. Lightly dip the damp sponge into the paint and then unload it by dabbing

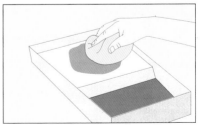

5 Pour the glaze into the roller tray and dip the sponge into the paint. Dab the excess paint onto the tray.

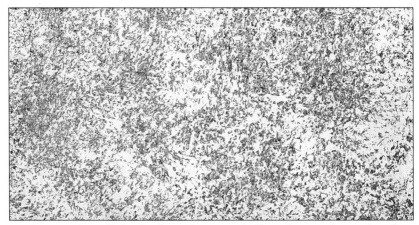

In close up, the wall clearly shows the sponged effect when an ultramarine glaze is applied over a mushroom base coat. This wall has had a second sponged glaze of yellow applied over the blue, but this is optional.

it on the slope of the tray. Test on a piece of paper to be sure the sponge is not overloaded—the print should show as fine spots.

6 Lightly dab the sponge over the base coated surface. If sponging a wall, print in panels about 1 m (3 ft) wide, fading out on the edges. Keep the sponge moving, turning it in every direction and lifting it cleanly off the wall. This way you will avoid skid marks and any repetitive impressions. Continue sponging until you have the coverage fairly even. Leave more of the mushroom base coat showing if you are going to apply more than one colour.

7 Continue sponging in successive panels, blending join marks between the panels as you work.

8 Allow the first colour to dry thoroughly before adding a second or third colour.

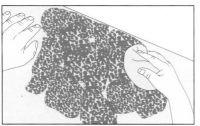

6 Using the sea sponge randomly apply the glaze over the base coat, turning the sponge in every direction.

HINT

When working on a large area such as a wall, stand back occasionally to check the work is even and not spotty. When sponging-on, it is better to cover the entire surface with one light coat first and check the overall effect before adding more glaze.

SUMMARY OF SPONGING AND RAGGING TECHNIQUES

SPONGING-ON

Sponging-on involves applying wet glaze to a base coated surface using a natural sponge. Usually, two or more colours are applied over the base coat to create a crisp, mottled effect. To ensure that your chosen sponged colours work well together, sponge them onto a board first to see the effect.

When selecting a sponge choose one with a crisp texture and with an uneven surface as this will give the best result. The straight lines of manufactured sponges tend to give a mechanical impression.

SPONGING-OFF

The sponging-off technique involves the partial removal of a wet glaze using a natural sea sponge. The glaze is applied with a large brush or roller over a base coated surface. The sponge is then dabbed over the glaze to partially remove it.

If working on a large area such as a wall, the sponging-off technique requires two people—the first person to apply the glaze, the second to remove the glaze with the sponge.

RAGGING-ON

Similar to sponging-on, except that the ragging-on technique uses a rag to apply the glaze. Scrunch the material into a ball and dip it into the glaze. Squeeze out the excess and dab it randomly over the base coated surface. Each time you refill the rag with paint undo it then scrunch it again to avoid a repetition of pattern.

RAGGING-OFF

Apply the glaze to the base coated surface and while the glaze is still wet, scrunch a piece of material or plastic into a ball and dab it over the surface to remove areas of the wet glaze. Constantly turn the pad to avoid a mechanical, repetitious look. Experiment with different materials to achieve variations in the texture.

RAG ROLLING-ON

Rag rolling-on involves using the rolled rag to apply glaze onto a base coated surface. Mix the glaze and pour it into a large paint tray. Roll the rag into a long sausage shape and roll it in the glaze. Squeeze out the excess glaze and roll the colour onto the surface, rolling the rag as you would a rolling pin.

RAG ROLLING-OFF

Rag rolling-off is very similar to ragging-off, except that the rag is folded into a sausage shape and rolled onto a wet glazed surface. This removes areas of the glaze to create a textured appearance.

Dragging

Dragging is a technique that produces a soft, subtle finish suited to walls but is also useful on small pieces such as picture frames or furniture. A stiff bristle brush is dragged through wet glaze to create an interesting texture of soft, fine lines.

METHOD

1 Prepare the surface (see General directions, page 9).

2 Apply two coats of light blue base colour to the prepared surface and allow the paint to dry thoroughly.

3 Mix the glaze using 1 part blue paint, 1 part scumble medium and 1 part water. Evenly brush the glaze over the entire surface.

4 With the stiff bristle brush in one hand and a dry rag in the other, firmly drag the brush through the glaze to create fine lines, exposing a little of the base colour. At the end of each pass, remove the excess paint from the brush by rubbing it in the cotton rag. This ensures you are removing paint and not just moving it around. Continue with parallel passes until the whole area is covered. Allow it to dry and add a darker painted blue border around the frame.

5 Apply one coat of satin varnish to finish. If the item will be exposed to wear, such as a table top or placemat, apply two to three coats of varnish to protect the painted finish.

MATERIALS

- Brush for base coat
- Water-based paint with a sheen: light blue, blue
- Acrylic scumble medium
- Brush for glaze
- Stiff bristle brush for dragging
- Cotton rags
- Small round brush for border
- Brush for varnish
- Water-based satin varnish (optional)
- Wall dragger or flogger (for large areas)

PAINTING LARGE AREAS

6 If you are working on a large area such as a wall, two people are required. The first applies the glaze in strips about 1 m (3 ft) wide; the second follows immediately behind with the dragging brush. When working on a large area use a special wall dragger, or flogger, about 35 cm (14 in) wide. The brush is dragged from the cornice to about two-thirds of the way down the wall, wiped off on a dry rag, and dragged from the skirting into the upper section. When finishing off, gently lift the brush away so that the brush strokes blend into the painted upper area.

To create a subtle effect such as that achieved on this picture frame, use two
shades of the one colour for dragging. Choose the glaze colour and lighten it
with white to create the base colour.

Dividing the wall into squares suggests the appearance of real blocks of marble. The glaze has been applied to each 'block' in a different direction to make the contrast between them stronger.

Plastic bagging (marble)

Depending on the colours you use, a plastic bagged glaze can suggest a marble or stone finish. Plastic bagging is very quick and few expensive tools are required, making it a versatile finish for decorative pieces or on a feature wall. This bagged marble finish is worked in large squares to create a 'blocked' effect.

MATERIALS

- Large brush for base coat
- Water-based paint with a sheen: white (base)
- Pencil and ruler
- Low-tack masking tape
- Artists' acrylic paints: Hooker's green, pthalo green, white (glaze)
- Acrylic scumble medium
- Large brush for glaze
- Cotton rags
- Plastic bags or kitchen cling film
- Brush for varnish
- Water-based satin varnish

METHOD

1 Prepare the surface (see General directions, page 9). As this technique is worked in 1 m (3 ft) squares, it can be completed by one person.

2 Using the large brush, apply two coats of white base colour to the prepared surface and allow the paint to dry overnight.

3 Mark out a 1 m (3 ft) square grid using a ruler and pencil. Lay masking tape around alternate blocks.

4 To make the glaze for marbling, first mix the paints as follows:
- 1 part Hooker's green
- 1 part pthalo green

Then mix the glaze using 1 part paint (as above), 1 part scumble medium and 1 part water.

5 Apply the glaze with the large brush and use the cotton rag to lightly dab over the glaze to break up the application marks.

6 Crumple the plastic then stretch it out so it forms folds. Lay it on the wet glaze and use the back of your hand to press it down—do not press with your fingertips. Lift off the plastic. Repeat the process, slightly varying direction and pressure as you

6 Crumple the plastic and then stretch it out so it forms soft folds. Lay it over the wet glaze.

PLASTIC BAGGING VARIATION

Achieve a slightly different effect using a black base coat.

1 Use a large brush and apply two coats of black paint to the surface.

2 To make the glaze, mix the paints as follows: 4 parts Hooker's green, 1 part pthalo green and 1 part white. Mix the glaze using 1 part paint, 1 part scumble medium and 1 part water.

3 Apply the glaze with the large brush and soften with a rag. Following steps 6–7, texture the

This finish uses a brighter green glaze over a black background.

glaze with a plastic bag. Allow it to dry. Following step 8, apply a paler green glaze.

4 Allow the glaze to dry and apply two coats of varnish.

cover the whole project. Discard the plastic as soon as it is covered in paint and start with a fresh piece. This will ensure that the paint is actually being removed and not just moved around.

7 Crumple the plastic into a soft ball and lightly pat it over areas to soften the impressions. Remove the tape as soon as the paint has begun to dry.

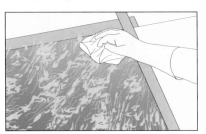

7 Crumple plastic into a soft ball and dab it over the wet glaze to soften the impression.

8 If you want to achieve a more subtle marbled effect, mix a second paler glaze by adding white paint to the existing mix of green paint. Proportions for this glaze should be 1 part paint, 2 parts scumble medium and 2 parts water. Brush this paler glaze over the work in drifts and immediately rag the surface with a ball of cotton cloth to remove most of the glaze, leaving a faint, uneven film.

9 When fully dry, mask the second set of blocks and repeat the glazing process. Vary the direction of the pattern so the blocks remain distinct. Continue this process until the wall is finished.

10 To finish the wall, apply two coats of satin varnish and allow it to dry.

MAKING AN IMPRESSION

In addition to the plastic used to create the plastic bagged marble finish, there are a variety of items found around the home that can create interesting impressions in a wet glaze.

The examples shown here are ideal for decorating frames, boxes or small pieces of furniture. Use the standard glaze of equal parts of acrylic paint, scumble medium and water (see step 4, page 51). If you don't like the effect, quickly repaint the surface with the glaze and try again.

FEATHER
Ruffle a large feather by drawing its edge between your thumb and forefinger. Wipe the feather through the glaze in a continuous zigzag motion to achieve an undulating impression in the glaze.

PAPER
For a fine impression tear a spare page from your telephone directory, crumple it into a tight ball and pat it over the wet glaze. The paper will absorb a little of the glaze to leave a crisp pattern.

CHAMOIS
Wet a small piece of chamois and wring it out until almost dry. Crumple the chamois in your hand and gently lift off the glaze. Turn the chamois about to vary the patterns in the glaze.

CARDBOARD
Use a ruler to tear a slightly uneven edge along a small piece of light cardboard. Hold the cardboard like a compass and wipe half circles through the glaze, overlapping them slightly.

Feather   *Paper*   *Chamois*   *Cardboard*

Plastic bagging (stone)

While walls make excellent surfaces for plastic bagging, smaller items such as a serving tray or this tissue box look effective when given a simple stone finish. This stone finish was created the same way as the marble wall finish but with a different coloured base coat and glaze.

METHOD

1 Prepare the surface (see General directions, page 9). If bagging a wall, wash it with water and soap to remove any dirt.

2 Using the large brush, apply two coats of the white base colour to the surface and allow it to dry.

3 To make the glaze, start by mixing the paint using 4 parts white and 1 part burnt umber. Then, mix the glaze using 1 part paint, 1 part scumble medium and 1 part water.

MATERIALS

- Large brush for base coat
- Water-based paint with a sheen: white (base)
- Artists' acrylic paints: white*, burnt umber (glaze)
- Acrylic scumble medium
- Large brush for glaze
- Cotton rags
- Plastic bags or kitchen cling film
- Brush for varnish
- Water-based satin varnish

(*house paint may be used)

4 Apply the glaze with the large brush and use the cotton rag to lightly dab over the glaze to break up the application marks.

5 Crumple the plastic and then stretch it out so it forms folds. Lay this on the wet glaze and run the back of your hand over it so the plastic rolls over the glaze. Lift off the plastic. Repeat the process, slightly varying the direction and pressure as you cover the whole project.

6 Crumple the plastic into a soft ball and lightly pat it over some areas to soften the impressions. Allow to dry.

7 For a more subtle effect, mix a second paler glaze. Proportions for this glaze are 1 part paint, 2 parts scumble medium and 2 parts water.

8 Brush this paler glaze over the work in drifts and rag the surface to remove most of the glaze, leaving just a faint, uneven film.

9 Allow the paint to dry overnight and apply two coats of satin varnish to finish.

Glazes and a plastic bagging technique have been used on this wooden tissue box to create the illusion that it is made from stone.

A colourwashed feature wall such as this adds freshness and light to a dark or tired room. The soft hues of the two green glazes team well with pinks, yellows and terracotta.

Colourwashing

Probably the fastest and easiest of the broken colour techniques, colourwashing can easily be achieved by one person. This finish looks best using two shades of one colour but experiment with a contrasting glaze for a more lively effect.

METHOD

1 When colourwashing it is important that the base coat be in matt water-based emulsion paint. This is to allow the glaze to absorb or adhere to the surface. If painting a wall, cover the floor with sheeting or newspaper as this glaze is quite runny. Prepare the surface for the paint finish (see General directions, page 9).

2 Paint the surface using two coats of light green base colour.

3 Mix the glaze using 1 part deep green paint, 2 parts scumble medium and 6 to 8 parts water.

4 Working quickly because of the absorbent background, apply the glaze using basketweave or broad,

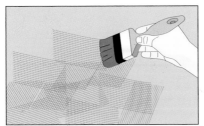

4 Use a large brush to apply the glaze to the wall using sweeping basketweave strokes.

MATERIALS

- Matt water-based emulsion paint: light green (base)
- Large brush for base coat
- Any water-based house paint: deep green (glaze)
- Acrylic scumble medium
- Large brush for glaze
- Cotton rags

curving sweeps. Use the rag to pick up any runs but otherwise, allow the brush marks to show. This results in a soft contrast between the lighter base and the darker glaze colour.

CHOOSING COLOURS

As the glaze for colourwashing is very transparent, choose a lighter or darker version of the base for a subtle effect, or a strong contrast for a lively effect. Remember, you will see the base colour showing through some areas so a blue wash over a red or pink base will appear violet in some parts and blue in others. Always experiment on a sample board first to see what effect you can expect when the job is finished.

Fresco effect

Fresco is a three-colour wall finish that suggests the faded look of Mediterranean houses. While tones of terracotta are popular, you can achieve a less traditional look by using any three colours, but whatever colours you choose, always make the first colour the darkest.

METHOD

1 Prepare the surface (see General directions, page 9). If painting a wall, cover the floor with old sheeting to catch any runs or splashes.

2 When this technique is used on walls it requires two people—the first applies the colour, the second follows behind softening the brush marks with a crumpled rag. Experiment using dry or slightly damp rags. A dry rag gives a slightly crisper impression than a damp rag. Smaller surfaces such as terracotta pots or small boxes require only one person.

3 Using the large brush, apply the terracotta paint in drifts (irregular shapes, loosely connected with lots of

MATERIALS

- Large brush for base coat
- Water-based paint with a sheen: terracotta, butter yellow, cream
- Soft cotton rags (cheesecloth, fine upholsterer's calico, muslin)
- Acrylic scumble medium
- Large brush for glaze

background showing). Use a slightly damp cotton rag to immediately soften the edges of the drifts and move a light film of colour over the exposed background. Allow the paint to dry for about two hours.

4 Make up the first glaze using 1 part yellow paint, 1 part scumble medium and 2 parts water.

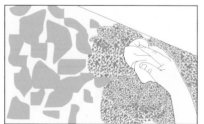

3 Apply the terracotta paint in drifts and use the damp rag to soften the edges of the paint.

HINT

On all wall finishes, avoid obvious overlaps where the panels of colour join by fading out the glaze towards the edges of the first panel and blending the wet edges of the second panel into the first. The overlaps are very difficult to disguise once the paint has dried.

A fresco effect wall finish adds personality to this room, the soft terracotta tones suggestive of the Mediterranean.

The first glaze (yellow) is applied over a terracotta base. A damp rag is then used to soften the brush marks and remove areas of the glaze.

The second glaze (cream) is applied, and again, a rag is used to soften and blend the glaze, exposing a little of the colours underneath it.

5 Using the glaze brush, apply the yellow glaze over the wall in panels about 1 m (3 ft) wide. The second person follows behind, dabbing over the wet glaze with a crumpled pad of damp rag, softening the brush marks and removing the glaze unevenly to expose the undercolour. Discard the rags into a bucket of water as they become clogged with paint and use a fresh rag. Allow the glaze to dry for about two hours.

6 Make up the second glaze with 1 part cream paint, 1 part scumble medium and 2 parts water.

7 Repeat the glazing and softening process following step 5. Rag the surface unevenly to allow all three colours to show, gently blended.

HINTS

- Applying paint effects, particularly on large areas, can be messy so it is advisable to wear old clothing and gloves.
- If decorating a wall, ensure the floor is covered with an old sheet or newspaper. Keep a rag nearby to wipe up any paint runs down the wall.
- If you are new to paint effects, and working on a large area such as a wall, it is a good idea to start the painting from an unobtrusive corner of the room (in a corner, behind a door or bookshelf). You will find that your technique will improve as you work around to the more prominent areas of the room.

Stencils

Rose stencil (page 41)

centre

Star stencil (page 22)

Stencil A

Adjust the size of
the stencil to suit

centre

Stencil B

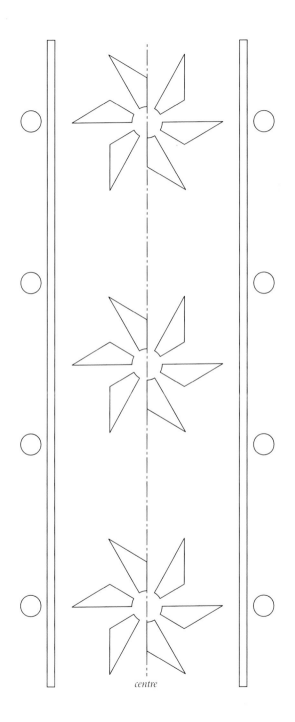

centre

Index